Prive Rooms

New poems by Mary N. Waters

the author of **Sandpaper Blankets**

Mary N. Waters

ISBN 0-9673137-1-6

You may e-mail the author at waters@aristotle.net

Cover painting:
 "Risk" by Charles Henry James

Design:
 H. K. Stewart

Sandpaper Press
4009 Kenyon Street
Little Rock, Arkansas 72205

Printed in the United States of America

Table of Contents

Acknowledgements

Once again, my love and gratitude to the wild, wise, and wonderful Wednesday women; also to the Spiritual Pilgrims, a group from whom I learn so much; H. K. Stewart, who wraps my words in beautiful packages; my family, for their love and support; and a special thank you to my grandson, Alex, who teaches us all to confront our fears.

"The sun gives us light, but the moon provides inspiration. If you look at the sun without shielding your eyes, you'll go blind. If you look at the moon without covering your eyes, you'll become a poet."

Serge Bouchard

Private Rooms

One day, while walking,
I saw a sign in a shop window:
"Help Needed," the sign said,
"Inquire Within,"
and I reflected that this is
a journey all of us will take
when we are ready;
when we come to know that
the strength, the grace,
the wisdom which we seek
"out there," await us in
the private rooms within,
all this; and so much more,
when we are ready.

Becoming

Sometimes I wonder what would happen
if I lost my "stuff";
the many, many material possessions
which I use to define myself
and distract me from
the real business of my life.
That I use the word "lost"
is no accident.
In so many ways, *losing* my stuff
would take the decision from my hands;
would make simplifying so much simpler.
But perhaps I am meant
to make some decisions,
to act from my deepest convictions,
to stop waiting for something
"out there" to take care of things;
to follow my heart and learn
to live the life that I was meant to live,
to give the gifts that I was meant to give;
to begin again now.

Leaflessons

Walking on a cool Fall morning,
I gathered leaves, so that I might
display them
throughout my house,
in honor of the season.
I held them carefully,
and as I looked
at what I had accumulated,
I felt such pride to see
the diversity of shapes and colors.
So should it be in life,
I thought;
people of all hues and sizes—
how lovely to be so open
to variety.
But then I looked again
at my charming bouquet,
and realized that it contained
no still-green leaves,
nor broken ones, with holes
or ragged edges; and
none grown dry,
pale-gray or brown with age.
Plurality was not represented
in my hand;
and so we learn life's lessons
on a cool Fall morning.

To My Son

Loving little boy,
smiling from photo albums,
sandwich filling between two sisters;
peacemaker in the family.
Now you are a grown man,
husband, father, son.

I know the difficulties
of being a woman in a
still-patriarchal world.
Often I have reflected
on the experience of men,
also heirs to the rules
of the patriarchy.
Are you allowed to speak your feelings,
to weep your sorrows,
to live your dreams?
Do you sometimes keep
a stiff upper lip
because you feel you must;
because the world expects it of you?
Times are changing now, for us all,
as we learn to grant ourselves permission
to abandon the old rules,

which no longer serve,
to remove the barriers,
as we move together, men and women
through light and shadow,
discarding duality,
embracing the Mystery,
growing into our hearts,
becoming the persons
we were meant to be.

Write Down the Dream

Write down the dream.
Preserve it for pondering,
let your mind play games with it,
unraveling a thread here and there;
moving the pieces of the puzzle about.
Trust your intuition, and
ask your heart for an opinion;
let it sink into your Self.
You may find answers
which will surprise you.

One

You have become the fabric
of my days and nights,
carried with me;
sometimes as a child
clutches her security blanket,
sometimes furtively,
stuffed into my knapsack,
so there will be no physical evidence
of my vulnerability.
Then there are those times
when I leave You behind,
needing to distance myself, because
I am angry,
or caught up in my own importance,
or in a dark place which I deem
undeserving of Your love.
Even then, I have come to sense
that I am never without You.
I no longer ask
"How can that be?"
Because my heart knows the answer
my head could never understand.

Learning to Listen

I wonder at the courage
that it takes
to learn to listen;
not to the world,
but to that still, small voice
which often seems to say
things which you want *so much* to hear,
that you are afraid to pay attention,
because you have grown up
in a world which says:
    Be obedient to those
    who want what's best for you;
    who are older,
    who are wiser,
    who make the rules.
    Rules which tell you to:
    Be humble,
    make sacrifices,
    be sensible,
    do your duty, and
    above all,
    follow the rules.
And yet, the voice is there.
It does not go away;
it is not loud,
rude,
angry.
It is simply there,

waiting;
knowing a secret
which it will share with you
if you have the courage
to listen
and to be...

Renegade

The paperwhite narcissus bulbs graced my home
with their fragrant blossoms.
Because they had grown very tall,
I tied them with raffia
to keep them from falling
in all directions.
But one linear leaf broke free,
unwilling to stand upright
according to my dictates.
Annoyed, I undid the restraining raffia,
and began again; on guard this time
for possible defectors.
Then, as I retied my bow, I reconsidered,
and loosened the shackles just a bit.
Soon, the same leaf
began a slow journey
toward its hermitage.
From time to time, I checked on its progress,
and found myself a silent cheerleader.
Today, mission accomplished,
the leaf had left the pack.
It made me smile, and,
more than that, it gave me hope,
that I might follow.

Emily's Song

There are people working to heal the planet;
visionaries who walk through this world,
who know its worn places
and wounded people,
yet see beyond
to other ways.
Their hearts are filled with reverence
for the earth and all its creatures;
its soil, forests, air and water;
for the gift of life.
Many heal through their own woundedness,
source, perhaps, of their compassion.
May we all learn to share their concern;
to know the healing energy of their caring.

Cosmic Hide-and-Seek

Now I know
there was a reason
I needed to discover
the game
as a small child;
the in-and-out,
up-and-down,
now-you-see-it,
now-you-don't,
game
of hide-and-seek.
It was to prepare me
for a lifetime;
for *many* lifetimes,
of searching.
Sometimes poised on the edge,
seeker not yet willing
to take the next step;
needing to withdraw,
to burrow into
a cave for a while;
at other times,
the one being sought
by the Mystery,
opening to it,
only to find that
it has disappeared.
Then I must become again

the searcher, exploring
other spaces, other places,
other ways.
Game without ending,
game without beginning,
cosmic circle-dance called
hide-and-seek.
How will I know when
I have come full circle?
I will simply know, as
the game resumes.

Growing into a Hermit's Life

My life is changing in many ways;
gossip sessions replaced by silence,
party-going replaced by solitude,
shopping trips replaced by inner pilgrimages.
And upon reflection, I find that
though I seldom miss my former pastimes,
I occasionally suffer an attack of the guilts
over my merciless abandonment of
that which I once held dear.
One thing for which I have not found
an antidote:
my compulsive need to "be there."
I know I still must learn
that there is no "there";
no magic destination to be won;
no coming in first or second, or even third;
no white, red or blue ribbons to be
proudly displayed upon my T-shirt.
And now…a few words about *control*;
about my need to be in it.
My head still tells me it is important
not to lose it,
not to give it up;
while my heart,
amused by this illusion,
has a good laugh at my expense.
So, though my life has changed
in many ways,

it seems there are more lessons
to be learned.
The good news, the very best news, is that
they are available, these lessons,
in every moment of my life,
and all I have to do is show up,
and open up, and pay attention, and...
Damn! I hear that sound of laughter again.   *25*

Flight to Minneapolis

Sitting next to you on the flight,
I didn't feel the usual:
"Oh, no, a mother and baby."
I thought perhaps it was because
I have grandchildren now,
and have become more empathetic,
but it was more than that.

I could tell you were a single mom,
and the lack of a wedding ring
wasn't a factor.
There was something about
the two of you, mother and son;
a kind of "It's you and me, kid,"
which didn't have to be spoken.
Later, I heard the story;
a trip to visit his father,
a month's stay planned,
which became only
a long weekend.
Still, I sensed a kind of relief
as you headed for home so far away,
with no plans to return.
And this I know for certain;
neither of you will ever lack for love,
as long as you are together.

Circle of Sisters

This small upper room, home
to our Wednesday gatherings;
our rituals and rememberings,
providing a container for
our tears and laughter;
a shelter for the sharing
of sorrows and blessings.
Patiently, through the heat
of summer, it awaits
the re-binding of ribbons,
the time when we
will sit again
in a circle;
a full-moon circle,
a circle of sisters.

Why?

Why do we teach our children
beliefs which we do not believe;
is it because they were taught to us,
and it is the only way we know?
Why do we think it important
for our children to learn
what they must only unlearn;
is it because we are afraid
to trust our heart in these matters?
How, then, will we come to wholeness,
and how will they;
if the cycle is not broken?

Liberation

At a time when joy was only
a dimmed memory, unable
to be summoned to the moment,
unable even to be longed for;
when questions were not met
by easy answers,
and the foundation of my life
lay crumbled,
bricks which had lost their mortar;
one connection remained,
a slender thread
to which I held, determined.
Its origin; a tapestry
woven of myths and memories
from all my years of living.
Perhaps this means the end, I thought,
but I held firm, and
with the tapestry's unraveling was born
a time of starting over, unencumbered,
a time of liberation from a past
to which I had been clinging,
and, most of all,
a time of transformation;
a new life story to be lived,
a vision to be honored.

Seeker

I needed some greenery
for a corner in my house,
but it was a dark corner,
and I didn't want a plant
which would shed its leaves
on my polished floor,
because there was so little light.

So I bought a silk ficus tree.
It looked so real that
unless one examined it closely,
it would be difficult to know
that my tree was not alive.
It seemed to me that after a while
its leaves began to reach toward the light.

My silk tree even had simulated dirt,
and I began to wonder
what would happen if
I were to water it.
Just a few drops at first,
and, gradually, a little more.
It was a bit messy.

There were some water spots on the floor.
They resisted polish.
One day I found a leaf
which had fallen from the tree.
Perhaps the water had loosened the glue.
Then I noticed a new shoot seeking the light,
and I smiled.

Numberology

One time I asked a group of women
how long it had been since,
for whatever reason,
their telephone number had changed.
This led to some interesting disclosures:
stories of divorce, relocation,
the need to request an unlisted number;
tales of job transfers, other opportunities,
old dreams replaced by new beginnings.
On and on the stories went.
Some of us, however, had kept
the same telephone number for
a very long time...
I wonder; does that mean
that we are stable...
or stuck?

Morning Walk

As I walked this morning, I noticed
a bed of flowers, waiting in the shade,
waiting for the sun's appearance,
confident of its arrival;
bringing growth.
Why is it, I wondered,
that I go to such lengths to avoid
so many of the things in my life
which would enable me to grow,
while the flowers wait
with such anticipation, such longing
for their opportunity?

Right-Brained Lament

I don't need a fax,
I don't want a modem.
I'd rather go back
and dance 'round a totem.

One Small Step for Mankind

"It's only your rational mind,"
I said;
"just conjuring up those scientific
facts and figures
again.
I don't think you should pay
much attention
to it.
Why not get into your imagination
instead?
That's the important place
to be;
the place where real learning
happens."
After a time, he smiled and said:
"I'll try."

Relief Map

Once upon a time, there was a little girl who was
responsible for everything.
It was a very big job, being responsible for
   everything,
but...that's not all.
When she grew up, she *continued* to be
responsible for everything, for a very long time,
until...one day she said:
"I no longer wish to be responsible for everything;
in fact...I no longer wish to be responsible
for much of anything."
And...clocks did not stop,
computers did not crash, (well, some did, but
that's not unusual on the best of days), and
birds continued to sing.
Now...we're just getting to the good part.
She put a lot of her stuff, including, but
not limited to, some pots and pans,
her watch,
seven "gift with purchase" lipsticks, never used,
an old china bowl which had belonged to Aunt
   Sophie
and everyone thought was ugly, but *someone* had to
   be responsible,
and twelve pairs of shoes,
at the curb with a sign. "Help yourself," the sign said,
"it's just stuff. But if you take too much of it,
you'll probably become (and here's that word again),

RESPONSIBLE, and if you do, I'm not responsible for it."
Now here we are, at the best part, the very best part:
the earth shook a little bit, and at first, people
    thought
it was maybe an earthquake, but it wasn't. Turns out,
it was just God breathing a huge sigh of relief.

Small Mistake; Large Lesson

She made a small mistake one day,
and threw out the contents
of a large basket, which was
full of my important stuff.
I guess she thought
it was a wastebasket
which needed to be emptied.
Well, that was
six months ago,
and I haven't really
missed anything that
was in that basket,
although at the time,
I was quite concerned.
I have given this incident
some thought, and concluded
that there are some other
areas of my life which
need to be emptied periodically,
and it will undoubtedly
be less painful
than I might imagine.

Do You Think?

Perhaps misanthropes
are simply people who
were meant to be hermits;
but didn't follow their bliss,
and now they, and everyone
in their lives
are paying the price
of their denial.

Source

In trying to learn
patience with others,
love, and compassion
for others,
I am finding that
it will not happen;
indeed, cannot happen,
until I have learned
to extend patience,
love and compassion
to myself.
That is the mouth
of the river;
the source
from which it flows.
That is a lesson which
I must learn and relearn,
moment by moment,
time after time.
Fortunately, I have a
patient, loving and
compassionate teacher,
if I will simply
pay attention.

Life

Life makes sense, it seems,
only to those who do not
expect it to;
to those who know,
or have learned,
not to beg a constant litany
of wheres, and hows
and whys and whens;
to those who have discovered that
there are no accidents.
While those who question everything
and always second-guess,
who've never learned to speak with spirits,
or to accept the Mystery,
often wear a puzzled look,
a life-makes-no-sense look;
a look I know, because
I've seen it in my mirror
more often than I'd like,
but not so often lately.

At Lakeside

Fog obscures the water
in the early hours of morning.
Light comes slowly,
cool energy arising.
Puffs and wisps
begin to separate
and float skyward.
I see the trees now
on the opposite shore;
showered by the fog,
cooled and cleansed by it,
they nod their thanksgiving.
Then, slowly, the water appears,
and day begins.

Invitation

I have, from the beginning,
been given an invitation
to be a co-creator with
the God who knows my name.
All my songs of praise and worship,
all my prayers of adoration;
these will matter very little,
if I have not paid attention,
if I have not sought my vision,
if my life's work remains undone.

Soulsense

To see without eyes,
to hear without ears,
to feel without touching,
and know the fragrance of jasmine,
although it does not bloom in my garden;
to taste old wine, and new, without consuming,
all this is possible, and more
with the understanding
that these are matters of the soul,
not simply of the senses.

Mid-Life

It seems to me
that I live
much of my life
in an in-between place.

I used to think
that there was
no middle ground,
no compromise.

I used to think
that things were
either black or white,
no muddled hues.

I used to think
that in-between
was no place at all.

Did I change because
I am more compassionate now,
or simply because
I have grown tired?

Two; Transformed

You sat there, so still,
your face turned away;
I wanted you to turn toward me.
Then, through the window, came
a light of such golden magnificence
that, turning toward it,
looking over my right shoulder,
I was changed forever.
"Look," I said, "at the light,"
but you did not move.
"Look," I repeated, half imploring,
half commanding, "look at the light."
And slowly, you turned
from that place where you had been
for a very long time,
and looked beyond me, to
that transforming light.

Housewear

As I look about my house of thirty years,
I see the faded paint in several rooms,
some carpet stains impervious to cleaning,
the nicks and scratches on the floors,
the worn places;
even some tooth marks on
the corner of the cabinet,
made by a set of tiny teeth,
a long, long time ago.
Later, glancing at the old hall mirror,
I smile to see
my house and I have grown old together,
both of us still standing proud,
despite the scrapes and dents and
wounded places;
perhaps, I think, because of them.

Power Animals:
The Shaman's Journey

The owl and the unicorn
greeted me as I descended,
their bodies gleaming white;
both eager to join me.
But I was unsure of their company,
particularly the owl,
for I had declared my intention
before beginning my journey:
to leave my head and dwell
in my heart.
And now, this owl had appeared,
symbol of wisdom, of the head
I wished to diminish.
"Ah," said the owl, sensing my concern,
"ah, but I am the wisdom of your heart."
And so we descended together,
an unlikely trinity.

Enough

The principle of scarcity
has come full circle;
what was illusion
has become reality.
Because of our fears
of not having enough,
we have taken and used
far more than we needed.
Where will we choose
to go from here?
Perhaps we no longer
have a choice.

There Are Days

There are days when I need grandmother God,
to rock me gently and tell stories from the past,
comforting stories; familiar to my heart.

At other times, I look for God the father,
to help me understand the ways of menfolk,
even though my father God is sometimes
just a bit confused by them Himself.

Mother God nourishes my body with food;
my soul with a lullaby-song,
on days when only that will do;
and teaches me of woman things.

For walking in the woods on autumn days,
I call on grandfather God, because
I love His reassuring presence,
His hand in mine; and mine in His.
He also teaches me about
the mystery of death.

Sister and brother God help me learn to share
all that has been provided in abundance,
and show me in so many gentle ways, that I, alone,
am not the center of the universe.

God the lover—oh! God the lover,
opens my heart to the wonder and the oneness
of us all; and also to the pain,
which is as much a part of it as joy.

And then there is my God the friend,
who answers all my questions honestly,
at times with truths I'd just as soon not hear,
but who is always, always there for me,
even when I think She's gone away.

Full-Filled

I am filled with solitude
and fulfilled by it.
I need my aloneness
as I need to draw breath;
a time of contemplation,
germination and revelation.
A time of in-dwelling,
of inner-knowing,
of transformation.
If others feel the pain
of loneliness,
I feel only the joy
of solitude,
returning me again and again
to the place I need to be.

Sometimes, A Smile

Sometimes, a smile
can be a touch,
a clasp of hands,
a warm embrace,
connecting us to the
beginningless,
endless,
Oneness.
If only for a moment,
by our transitory measure,
a smile becomes
everything we need.

Release

Where are your feelings?
In what far-off place do they exist;
hidden, dormant, buried?
Do they want you to find them,
and befriend them?
I think that you would be surprised
how good it would feel
to give them some exercise,
allow them to bend and stretch,
and roll around;
perhaps do a dance of wonder
and joyous release.
Are you afraid that,
once released,
they would not go back
into their box,
and you would lose control?

Circle Dance

Many of us dance together
to the drumbeat
at the center
of the circle.
Some venture out
to a place
where, often,
they must dance
without a partner,
straining to hear
the distant drums.
Still others
find the edge,
where they dance
accompanied by a drumbeat
only they can hear;
alone,
but not lonely.

Women Who Weep

Who are the women who weep?
Do they weep for all humanity, and
does their caring connect us?
Do their tears contain wisdom, which
will replenish our rivers?
As their tears flow deep
into the earth, do they heal
the battlegrounds
and barren places?
Who are the women who weep?
If we listen to their tears, will
our souls hear, and
will we remember?

Missionary Work

Missionaries filling the world with their fervor;
their external quest to convert others,
to win their souls,
are very frightening to me.
Why do they want to change others;
have they finished working on themselves?
And do they not understand that other souls
are not theirs to win, like a carnival prize?

I am learning to become
a missionary on an *internal* quest;
at times a difficult journey,
this much-needed traveling to my center;
this mission trip to my Self.
I can always find work to be done there;
voices to be heard, changes to be contemplated.
Upon my return, I am pleased to discover
that my inward travels have kept me far too busy
to worry about the souls of my sisters and brothers.
And therein lies the true blessing for all
whom I meet along the way.

A Daughter's Question

Instead of asking "why?"
You ask me what
you are meant to learn
from your firstborn.
I turn the question
back to you.
After some deliberation,
you reply
"I think maybe patience...
maybe...compassion."
And I, uncharacteristically
at a loss for words, respond
"Well, that ain't bad, kid,
that ain't bad."

Saving Grace

My Grandmother saved things;
prettily embroidered dishtowels,
fancy tablecloths and napkins,
linen handkerchiefs,
a string of pearls;
all tucked away in dresser drawers,
and dining room buffets,
and jewelry cases,
awaiting a very special occasion;
some exceptional occurrence,
which never seemed to
actually occur.
"What are you saving it for?"
someone would ask,
and Grandmother would smile,
and say "Oh, someday…"
I used to laugh about it,
until I realized that
what my Grandmother was doing
with her handkerchiefs and pearls,
I was doing with my life.

Candles

There are many candles in my life.
Some provide light for my journey;
others go far beyond,
and illuminate me; enabling me
to see my own light,
helping me to know
who I am, and
why I am here.
They share their steady light
when mine is wavering ,
teaching me to connect with
all the candles in my life,
no matter their color, size or shape;
no matter if their flame
is strong or fragile, dim or bright,
inviting me to be that light for others,
as we discover the Oneness.

C. P. Remembered

He slept at the sawmill,
in a pile of shavings,
my father said.
He'd had a hard life,
and some of his relatives
were, perhaps, a bit ashamed.
Early one morning, my father
got a call.
61
When he returned, he said that
C. P. had died during the night,
in his pile of shavings.
I remember my father
making a point about
how clean C. P. was—
his body; his underwear.
"So clean," he said, and,
"He was a good man,
who had some troubles."
Now, more than fifty years later,
I think of this, and add:
As are we all.
As do we all;
which, I think, is exactly
what my father had in mind.

Sara

To hear another voice,
one familiar, and yet strange;
to see a face
which is not my face,
(the one I see in the mirror, anyway),
is not disturbing to me.
Puzzling, perhaps, but
I am not afraid
to call upon her,
to ask questions,
to listen to her advice,
and know a face and voice
which come to me from
depths within.
This is to know possibilities
I had only wished for,
to access wisdom
old as my soul,
to learn from shadows
from which I used to hide; and,
because their time has come,
I unearth their roots;
some very deep,
and replant them
in the light.

M'Aleese and Me

A year goes by, and once again
we meet for lunch, our Scorpio celebration,
always a smooth transition from the year before.
This is our time, to tell our past-year stories,
hearing words both spoken and unspoken,
each seeing through the other's eyes;
eyes sometimes sparkling with laughter,
sometimes shining with tears.
Quietly, we reflect upon the way it has been for us,
knowing we have created a safe space
in our corner of the restaurant,
content in each other's company once again.

Core Within

There is a core
within me,
offering support,
even when
I do not ask;
perhaps *especially* then.
I had always imagined
it to be
made of steel,
this core;
or stone,
or granite.
But now I know
that it is none
of these.
My core is simply
made of light.

Andy's Word

"Meanship" is a very appropriate word;
a strong word; a powerful word.
Because, after all,
if there can be friendship,
then there can be an opposite word,
and I can't think of one more suitable
than meanship.
So from now on, when I encounter
someone who doesn't want to be my friend,
or share his toys, or play nicely,
I will think of your word, and know
that it also applies to me at times.
Perhaps someday, if we're very lucky,
we won't need the word anymore,
but the way things are now,
I'm afraid it is very much needed,
so thank you, Andy,
for teaching it to us.

The Point

The deer have come,
and eaten the plants
which we have tended
throughout the summer.
My first thought is
that something must be done;
sprays, perhaps, or moth balls;
strange brews or potions
which will alarm, or at least
discourage them.
But what is the point
of all that?
Summer is ending;
the plants are gone
a bit before their time,
or are they?
Life continues
to teach us lessons
as slowly, we learn
to pay attention.

Just a Suggestion

Life holds frequent
surprises for us,
on a rather
erratic schedule.
Hummm...can a
"schedule" be erratic?
At any rate,
I have learned
that when everything
appears to be
coming up roses,
it's probably not
a good idea
to throw away
the weed-eater.

Opportunity

I used to think it was lovely
when I heard or read that
inconveniences were
simply opportunities,
put on our path in order
for us to learn life lessons.
I probably even said it myself,
on occasion.
But now that I *believe* it,
it's become a whole new ballgame.
It hasn't made my life any easier,
but...
I'm learning some interesting lessons;
oh yeah! Some very interesting lessons.

Final Curtain

There are many ways
for relationships to end;
in anger or in relief,
a shout or a whisper,
clarity or confusion,
sadness, or simply weariness.
Perhaps relationships
do not end at all,
but are simply deferred
to another lifetime.

Sanctuary

Here I sit,
right foot wrapped
in an elastic bandage,
propped on a pillow,
ice bag in place;
resting, ice-ing, compressing, elevating,
as the hastily consulted

First Aid manual suggests.
"Not a good time"; I think,
"things to do, places to go;
won't be driving for a while—damn!"
Then I allow a thought
which I've been keeping way out
on the edge of awareness:
Is there a lesson in this;
happening so soon after the start
of the new year?
I don't remember any resolutions about
strains or sprains or bruises.
A small voice prompts:
"Well, it's the season for quiet contemplation,
for hibernating in the sanctuary of self,
letting go, by trading, perhaps, the 'to do' lists
for some 'to don'ts.'"
"Okay," I bargain, trying my best to smile
like a good sport, "and if I learn this lesson,
could I possibly…" Never mind, I know the answer,
or at least I'm beginning to, as I hobble toward

lesson number 7,826,
or perhaps it's lesson number one trillion—
waiting right down the road, waiting for me;
unpredictable, yet exactly as planned.

Food Triptych

I.

In a world where
people are starving,
it seems that I
have a full plate, but
I don't like
any of the food.
Could it be that I
am the one
who is starving?

II.

Perhaps I need to go on a diet;
one which will enable my spirit
to fly free; unencumbered by
all this weight,
which keeps it from flights of fancy,
and makes it a prisoner,
trapped in the mashed potatoes
of my life.

III.

I am addicted to potato chips,
and pretzels and nuts,
so when I hear someone say;
"always make your words sweet and tender,
for tomorrow, you may have to eat them,"
I can only respond that
I prefer salty food, and
luckily, I have strong teeth.

Alex

Alex, little golden boy,
how hard it is for us
to understand
the part of you
that lives in shadows.
But darkness can nourish
as well as light,
and as you begin to emerge,
you will carry the strength
of the shadow,
and it will serve you well.
We have lessons to learn
from you;
far greater, I think,
than those you will learn
from us.

Remembering

When the search began,
I do not know.
In this lifetime,
it has intensified
with my understanding that
a day of receptivity
is more valuable than
a lifetime of asking questions.
I am remembering my daughter's
little dog, Tigger,
who loved to give kisses.
Sometimes, Kathie would be moved
to say: "Too many kisses, Tigger,
too many kisses."
There are times when I think
God must be telling me:
"Too many questions, Mary,
too many questions."

Mindful

To live in the present moment
is my goal, but first
I need to process what happened
at the meeting yesterday,
and think about the menu
for Bruce's birthday dinner.
There are some bills which need
to be paid; I should have done that
earlier this week; and I have
a dental appointment tomorrow,
and some things to drop off
at the cleaners...
So, though I truly want
to live mindfully,
I'm afraid that my mind is
already full.

Down to Earth

Mary:
woman of passion and fire;
who dressed you in blue and white?
Where is the red in your wardrobe?
The green?
The sparkle in your eyes?
How did you get kicked upstairs to corporate,
when you wanted only to be in the trenches?
To dig in the soil,
and grow some herbs and cabbages,
perhaps plant tulip bulbs and daffodils,
and feel the dirt under your fingernails,
and smell the damp earth beneath your hands.
Who put that crown upon your head,
which falls off each time you bend
to embrace a small child?
Who cast your eyes upward, calling you
Queen Of Heaven, making eye contact with
ordinary folks like me so difficult?
Serene woman, I know your feet long to dance
to the rhythm of the cosmos—
take off your veil, and,
with a polite smile, hand it
to the patriarchy, saying:
"Thank you, gentlemen, but I must be
moving on now. Feel free to join me,
if you wish."
And then, put on your dancing shoes,
or, better yet, go barefoot.

Seemed to Me

It seemed to me that
once you figured out
where you came from, and
where you are going, and
that there are reasons for all
the encounters,
the stops and starts,
and detours,
in between;
well, it seemed to me that
then should come peace,
and contentment, and
understanding, but;
can you believe it?
That is only the beginning…

Begin

Sing your life,
dance it
with passion
in each new moment,
each now moment.
You know the words
to your Lifesong.
Go within,
and find them
written on your soul.
You know the steps
to your Lifedance.
They are waiting
in your heart.
Open it,
and dance the steps;
be danced by them
with each new heartbeat,
each now heartbeat.
Your song.
Your dance.
Begin.

About the Author

Mary Waters grew up in Northern Wisconsin and now lives in Little Rock, Arkansas. She is the author of a previously published book of poetry, *Sandpaper Blankets*. One of the poems in that book, "Out of the Box," got her off the Conformity Bus, and she's been enjoying the journey (especially the detours) ever since.